Copyright © 2021 by Tamika Hill

All rights reserved. This book or any portion thereof may not be reproduced or used in any manner whatsoever without the expressed written permission of the publisher except for the use of brief quotations in a book review.

Nothing contained in this book should be construed as legal advice.

Printed in the United States of America

ISBN:
978-0-578-87472-2

Manifest Your Vision Planner

"A vision is only a dream until the day you meet the goals that are required toaccomplish it."

–THILL

Manifest Your Vision Planner

This is not just another planner; it is the guideline to help you manifest your vision. Every year we create vision boards, but if we are honest with ourselves how much of the vision board do we manifest into our reality? Now understand, I believe in vision boards because most people are visual. However, after you have found all the motivational quotes, pictures, and letters - what is the plan? Every vision requires a plan. Every plan requires direction. Every direction requires step by step instructions.

This planner is divided into four quarters to help break down your vision into manageable goals designed to be obtainable for you. Each quarter has three months and within those three months are 30-60-90 day goals with weekly steps you will write down to accomplish those goals. These can be smaller goals broken down into steps to get you closer to meeting your "big" or long-term goal for the year. For example, if your long-term goal is to repair your credit, a quarterly goal may be to have one debt paid off each quarter. Your monthly goal may be to pay incrementally towards a targeted debt on your credit. A weekly goal may be to create a budget for the week. Remember a vision is built in small stages, step by step. Another example is maybe you want to start your own company; a weekly goal can include things like research to create a mission statement, assessing other companies similar to your business, and developing a name. A quarterly goal may be to have a name for your company and create a mission statement. Another quarterly goal may be creating a budget for your start up costs.

The key is to remember that when planning out your goals you must practice patience. Do not be over ambitious. Do your research. Do not be afraid to ask questions or make mistakes, you are human. Make sure you are ready to invest in yourself as well as your vision. Do not compete with anyone. This is your vision - not a competition.

Manifest Your Vision Planner

Before we start, we need to understand the definition of the terms we will be using in this planner:

Manifest - It is the ability to make something come to pass or certain by showing or displaying it.

Vision - Something that is conceived or seen, maybe through a concept or a dream.

Planner – A person or thing (journey, notebook) that plans something, put things into a task form.

Goal - The end towards which an effort a person or objective is directed to.

Measurable - The ability to be able to be described in specific terms for example as of duration, or time usually expressed as a quantity in numbers (we will use this concept by measuring our goals in weeks, months, and quarters)

Obtainable – To establish or gain by a plan of action or effort on one's part.

Manifest Your Vision Planner

I recommend that you have no more than five goals at a time because you do not want to get overwhelmed trying to accomplish too much at once. For my over achiever, you do not want to put so many goals on your plates that you do not enjoy and learn the valuable lessons on the journey. For my procrastinator, you want to use the goal chart to keep you on track. Your goals should be strategic and realistic to your vision. We want to make measurable goals so that they really are obtainable.

- Long term goals - These are goals that will take more time to accomplish in a year or more.

- Mid quarter goals - These are goals to be met in 6 months.

- Quarterly goals - These are goals that will be met in 90 days.

- Monthly goals - These are small goals that can be met in 30 days.

- Weekly goals - These are smaller goals you will do for each week.

Are you Ready to Manifest your vision? If yes, then let us get to work.

Manifest Your Vision Planner

First Step

Before you write down the goals to manifest your vision, here is a list of questions to ask yourself:

1. What are the reasons why you want to manifest your vision?

_____

_____

_____

(This is important to Remember because - When you are ready to give up on your vision this will be your WHY/REASONS you will not and cannot quit).

2. When you manifest your vision into your reality – what purpose will it serve?

_____

_____

_____

3. Who will your vision serve? Will it be just you, your family, the community, the nation, or the world?

_____

_____

_____

Manifest Your Vision Planner

(Remember no vision is too big to manifest. We just need to make and meet the goals to achieve the vision. Consistency is Key.)

4. What will change for you?

_____
_____
_____

5. What will change for your family?

_____
_____
_____

6. Will it change the generation?

_____
_____
_____

7. Who will support you to help achieve this vision?

_____
_____
_____

Manifest Your Vision Planner

Second Step

Identify an accountability partner and a support team.

This is one of the most important steps. Why? Well, most visions do not come to manifestation because there is no one helping us to be accountable for what we say. Yes, this is your vision, but a goal is never met alone. It always requires a team of support. Make sure your accountability partner is capable of what you require of them. Do not pick a person who will not challenge you on your road to manifesting your vision; you will need people to challenge you despite the barriers or obstacles you will face.

_____

_____

_____

_____

Your support team should be people who can encourage you, inspire you and help keep you motivated on your journey to manifesting your vision. They can also be people who can assist you with different tasks or revealing information you need on this journey. Make sure the people on your support team are not secret haters or vision snatchers. You will have enough obstacles on this journey. Do not let your support team be one of them. Choose wisely.

_____

_____

_____

_____

Manifest Your Vision Planner

Third Step

Alright, now that you have your WHY and your team, let's write the Long-term Vision – for the year. Remember, if you work the vision it will come to fruition.

Create a Mini Vision Board 1st Quarter (January – March)

Fourth Step

Alright, now that you have your WHY, your team, your Mini Vision board for the first quarter – let's write the Long-term Vision for the year.

Remember, if you work the vision it will come to fruition.

_____

_____

_____

_____

Step Five

What will be your Mid Quarter Goal (6-month mark)?

Remember, when you meet this goal, you are halfway there, so let's dig deep. Do not turn back now. You have come too far to quit!

_____

_____

_____

_____

Manifest Your Vision Planner

Step Six

Now that you have your long-term goal and mid quarterly goal, what will be your first month goal? Let's get started.

What is your first monthly goal (30-day mark)? Let's make sure you make this a realistic and obtainable goal. You have 11 more months to go so do not rush the process.

_____
_____
_____
_____
_____
_____
_____
_____

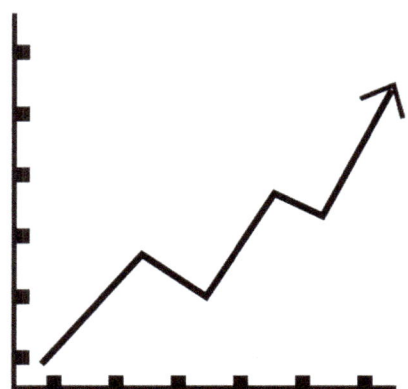

Manifest Your Vision Planner

"Remember, a road you never travel is one less place you will not see. So, let us be adventurous and explore the different roads! They just may lead you to manifest your vision."

–THILL

Vision Board Page

Quarter 1

Quarter One Goals

30 Days

1. _____

   _

2. _____

60 Days

1. _____

   _

2. _____

90 Days

1. _____

   _

2. _____

Goals Set Up

This is the beginning phase to start manifesting your vision.

DATE / /

WEEK OF / /

Monday

Tuesday

Wednesday

Thursday

Friday

Are you still on track, if not no sweat? Do not be too hard on yourself it is still only the Beginning phases and You are learning the process.

DATE / /

WEEK OF / /

Goals Set Up

Monday

Tuesday

Wednesday

Thursday

Friday

Goals Set Up

Remember, you are almost at the 30-day mark.

DATE
WEEK OF   /   /
            /   /

Monday

Tuesday

Wednesday

Thursday

Friday

Goals Set Up

Now before you go writing all these goals down, review what strategies worked last time and review what strategies did not work not and implement that information into your goals.

DATE __/__/__

WEEK OF __/__/__

Monday

Tuesday

Wednesday

Thursday

Friday

Goals Set Up

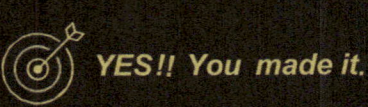 *YES!! You made it.*

DATE   /   /

WEEK OF   /   /

Monday

Tuesday

Wednesday

Thursday

Friday

Manifest Your Vision Planner

YAY!!!

The first 30 days completed.

WOW! You hit your first 30 days.

*****Alright, drum-roll please, did you meet your 30-day goal(s)? *****

Review: What was your 30-day goal(s)?

How are you feeling about your progress?

_____
_____
_____
_____

If you did not meet your goal(s) review what strategies worked over the past few weeks and what did not work.

_____
_____
_____
_____

Manifest Your Vision Planner

Are your goal(s) realistic and obtainable in the amount of time allotted for the week and month? Y / N (circle answer)

Do you need to challenge yourself and dig deeper if the goal(s) are too easy? Y / N (circle answer)

Are your goal(s) still in alignment with meeting your quarterly goal(s)? Y / N (circle answer)

Let us check in with your accountability partner/team.

Make sure to review your answers with your accountability partner.

Goals Set Up

Let us make sure to make this week goals realistic and obtainable You have 11 more months.

DATE / /

WEEK OF / /

Monday

Tuesday

Wednesday

Thursday

Friday

Goals Set Up

Do not rush the Process.

DATE   /   /

WEEK OF   /   /

Monday

Tuesday

Wednesday

Thursday

Friday

Goals Set Up

Let us make sure we make this is a realistic and obtainable goal. We You have 11 more months to go so do not rush the process.

DATE   /   /

WEEK OF   /   /

Monday

Tuesday

Wednesday

Thursday

Friday

Goals Set Up

Let us make sure we make this is a realistic and obtainable goal. We You have 11 more months to go so do not rush the process.

DATE   /   /

WEEK OF   /   /

Monday

Tuesday

Wednesday

Thursday

Friday

Goals Set Up

Let us make sure we make this is a realistic and obtainable goal. We You have 11 more months to go so do not rush the process.

DATE / /

WEEK OF / /

Monday

Tuesday

Wednesday

Thursday

Friday

Manifest Your Vision Planner

YAY!!!

The first 60 days are completed.

WOW! You hit your first 60 days.

*****Alright drum-roll please, did you meet your 60-day goal(s)? *****

Review: What was your 60-day goal(s).

How are you feeling about your progress?

_____

_____

_____

_____

If you did not meet your goal(s) review what strategies worked over the past few weeks and what did not work.

_____

_____

_____

_____

Manifest Your Vision Planner

Are your goal(s) realistic and obtainable in the amount of time allotted for the week and month? Y / N (circle answer)

Do you need to challenge yourself and dig deeper if the goal(s) are too easy? Y / N (circle answer)

Are your goal(s) still in alignment with meeting your quarterly goal(s)? Y / N (circle answer)

Let's check in with your accountability partner/team.

Make sure to review your answers with your accountability partner.

Goals Set Up

Let us make sure we make this is a realistic and obtainable goal. We You have 11 more months to go so do not rush the process.

DATE / /

WEEK OF / /

Monday

Tuesday

Wednesday

Thursday

Friday

Goals Set Up

 Let us make sure we make this it is a realistic and obtainable goal. We You have 11 more months to go so do not rush the process.

DATE / /

WEEK OF / /

Monday

Tuesday

Wednesday

Thursday

Friday

Goals Set Up

 Let us make sure we make this is a realistic and obtainable goal. We You have 11 more months to go so do not rush the process.

DATE / /

WEEK OF / /

Monday

Tuesday

Wednesday

Thursday

Friday

Goals Set Up

Let us make sure we make this is a realistic and obtainable goal. We You have 11 more months to go so do not rush the process.

DATE ___/___/___

WEEK OF ___/___/___

Monday

Tuesday

Wednesday

Thursday

Friday

Goals Set Up

Let us make sure we make this list is a realistic and obtainable goal. We You have 11 more months to go so do not rush the process.

DATE / /

WEEK OF / /

Monday

Tuesday

Wednesday

Thursday

Friday

Manifest Your Vision Planner

YAY!!!

The first 90 days are completed. Quarter 1 completed.

WOW! You hit your first 90 days.

*****Alright drum-roll please, did you meet the 90-day goal(s)? *****

Review: What was your 90-day goal(s)?

How are you feeling about your progress?

_____
_____
_____
_____

If you did not meet your goal(s) review what strategies worked over the past few weeks and what did not work.

_____
_____
_____
_____

Manifest Your Vision Planner

Are your goal(s) realistic and obtainable in the amount of time allotted for the week and month? Y / N (circle answer)

Do you need to challenge yourself and dig deeper if the goal(s) are too easy? Y / N (circle answer)

Are your goal(s) still in alignment with meeting your quarterly goal(s)? Y / N (circle answer)

Let's check in with your accountability partner/team.

Make sure to review your answers with your accountability partner.

Goals Set Up

 Let us make sure we make this is a realistic and obtainable goal. We You have 11 more months to go so do not rush the process.

DATE   /   /

WEEK OF   /   /

Monday

Tuesday

Wednesday

Thursday

Friday

Goals Set Up

Now before you write these goals down review what worked and did not work last week.

DATE   /   /

WEEK OF   /   /

Monday

Tuesday

Wednesday

Thursday

Friday

Goals Set Up

Now before you write these goals down review your monthly goal, are you closer to reaching that goal?

DATE / /

WEEK OF / /

Monday

Tuesday

Wednesday

Thursday

Friday

Goals Set Up

 *Remember, you are almost at the 60-day mark. Let's make this these next few weeks count.*

DATE ___/___/___

WEEK OF ___/___/___

Monday

Tuesday

Wednesday

Thursday

Friday

Goals Set Up

Remember, you are almost at the 60-day mark. Let's make this these next few weeks count.

DATE __/__/__

WEEK OF __/__/__

Monday

Tuesday

Wednesday

Thursday

Friday

Manifest Your Vision Planner

"You are making strides towards manifesting your goals so do not disregard small beginnings because it will create big opportunities in the long run. Keep up the good work. It takes time to manifest a vision remember that."

—THILL

Vision Board Page

Quarter 2

Manifest Your Vision Planner

Quarter Two Goals

30 Days

1. _____

    _

2. _____

60 Days

1. _____

    _

2. _____

90 Days

1. _____

    _

2. _____

Manifest Your Vision Planner

"It may seem like you are not progressing in your journey and the process seem so repetitive, however small changes occur with consistent behaviors which lead to major changes. Hang in there."

—THILL

Vision Board Page

Quarter 3

Manifest Your Vision Planner

Quarter Three Goals

30 Days

1._____

2._____

60 Days

1._____

2._____

90 Days

1._____

2._____

Manifest Your Vision Planner

"No matter what you accomplished or did not accomplish remember you are still moving forward in the journey. Because you made the decision to manifest your Vision, it's no longer a dream. You have met some goals, but maybe not all the goals you would have liked to meet, just remember to be patient and kind with yourself. It is not a race it is a vision; remember, visions take time to manifest. Now go rest and reset for the next final 2 quarters."

-*THILL*

Quarter 4

Vision Board Page

Manifest Your Vision Planner

Quarter Four Goals

30 Days

1. _____

2. _____

60 Days

1. _____

2. _____

90 Days

1. _____

2. _____

Manifest Your Vision Planner

"Congratulations you made it. You have manifested your Vision. Even when the road got bumpy, and you had to take detours you stay the course to Manifest the Vision. It was not easy if you be honest but celebrate the fact you overcame the obstacles despite of everything you faced. Sometimes you had to go back re-write Some things, research some more, cry, fail so you could learn a new way and even felt alone. But Never give glory to the struggle but magnify the fact you Manifest the Vision. You took a chance on you and you WON… Always fight hard for you because YOU MATTER. YOUR VISION MATTERS.
Remember this from this day forward you have what it takes to Manifest Your Vision so NEVER GIVE UP ON YOU."

—THILL

www.ingramcontent.com/pod-product-compliance
Lightning Source LLC
Chambersburg PA
CBHW061759290426
44109CB00030B/2896